Out of Silence

Acknowledgements

Out of Silence
New & Selected Poems
John Harvey

smith|doorstop

Published 2014 by
smith|doorstop Books
The Poetry Business
Bank Street Arts
32-40 Bank Street
Sheffield S1 2DS
www.poetrybusiness.co.uk

ISBN 978-1-910367-01-8

British Library Cataloguing-in-Publication Data.
A catalogue record for this book is available from the British Library.

Typeset by Utter
Printed by Printondemand.com
Cover image: © Molly Boiling
Author photo: © Molly Boiling

smith|doorstop Books is a member of Inpress,
www.inpressbooks.co.uk. Distributed by Central Books Ltd.,
99 Wallis Road, London E9 5LN.

The Poetry Business is an Arts Council
National Portfolio Organisation

Supported by
**ARTS COUNCIL
ENGLAND**

Contents

Bluer Than This

for Molly

New Poems

Saturday

Having slept through
the entire Cup Final
our daughter stumbles
blearily into the room
eyes wild and hair askew
demanding food.

A family of foxes
two adults and three stubby cubs
is living in our garden
littering it with waste and bones.

Frances died, Jim,
after thirty five years of marriage.
When we were teenagers
you used to call across
the room we shared
"Good night, John,
  and God Bless."

This evening at the Vortex,
shoulder hunched and
greying hair brushed back,
Stan Tracey, well past seventy,
fingers percussive and strong,
played Monk's 'Rhythm-a-Ning'
scuttling crab-like across the keys
and I thought of her and you
and all there was between
you. Interlocked.

This then is what we do,
the only thing we can,
sometimes solo,
sometimes hand in hand:
forward, sideways,
sideways, back.

The Light This Morning
for Nancy Nielsen

The light this morning is touching everything
the poet says, and I imagine you
standing tall again
no longer numbed or navvied
by pain
letting loose the dogs
then stepping with them
into the pearl of early morning
the dew on the grass
fresh around your feet

I see you
walking in this early light
bending to your garden
setting things to rights
these moments before
the day itself is up and going
a tune somewhere playing
in memory
a song someone in your family
is singing one carefree afternoon
the windows carelessly open
the melody drifting away

The light this morning touches everything
purple, gold and crimson
piercing the richness
of trees
the twist and turn of grasses
and the call of birds
whose names come to you
almost as your own

A bird starts up from the trees
and you turn towards its call;
already there are fishermen
at work in the bay,
their voices
rise and fall

A moment
then you turn
back towards the house
the cool of the kitchen
smell of coffee newly ground
the small clear crack of shell
as the eggs are loosed into the bowl
apples sliced straight into the butter
foaming ready in the pan
flour
a dusting of sugar
cinnamon:
Apple Schmarren

The taste of it,
the cabin encircled
almost, by trees
the clearing into which we walked,
and you walked out to greet us
the light around us touching everything

Your poet's eye
your gaze
your stubborn hardiness and grace.

Apparently
for Matthew Caley

Apparently, James Butler Hickok
and William Butler Yeats
shared more than just a common middle name.
It's a little known fact but true
that on the sole occasion
Yeats foreswore his habit of a lifetime,
borrowed from Wild Bill, and sat
with his back to the batwing doors,
an earnest young gunslinger,
out to make a name for himself,
kicked them open and beat Yeats,
hands down, to the last two lines
of '*The Lake Isle of Innisfree*'.

Poem
(In Imitation of Frank O'Hara)

The rain is falling,
　　lightly
the way it did for Frank
when he stepped out onto the sidewalk
that would take him to St. Mark's Place;
Camels, two packs, in his pockets,
a notebook; nothing more on his mind
than a quick espresso on Bleecker or MacDougal,
meeting maybe Grace or Jane,
before riffling through the pre-loved books
– though he wouldn't have called them that, of course –
outside the bookstores on Fourth Avenue
in search of some hidden gem.
　　What was it?
Whatever the poets in Ghana are up to these days.

But here, the rain falling heavier now,
verily, it pisseth down so hard
the cat will no more push her nose outside
than she would swivel round and present
her more than elegant backside to the world
　　and I wonder
what another espresso would do to my metabolism,
remembering that morning on my way back
from shooting the breeze with Norbert Hirschhorn,
health hero, friend, and grand poet of the Lebanon,
when, after downing two double-shot lattes
in quick succession, I left him at the bus stop
and suddenly this pain like a giant foot
stepped down on my heart and, winded,
　　I stopped in my tracks
sweating and fearful at the thought of it all ending

so close to where we used to catch, my daughter and I,
the C11 bus to the library,
but then, as I rested, the pain began to fade
and with it my fears and with scarcely a wave
in whatever direction Bert had taken,
I continued home to where I am now,
sitting at the window, waiting for the rain to cease
so that I can go out for my morning walk
and wondering, in the meantime,
should I listen again to the Berg Violin Concerto
that has just stopped playing or simply sit
and leaf through this beautiful little Tibor de Nagy edition
of O'Hara's poems, the one with Larry Rivers drawings
and Grace Hartigan's gorgeous painting of *Oranges*?
    How my heart leapt
that morning not so long ago
when I walked into the poetry room at Foyles
and saw it there, face out, among the new acquisitions,
just begging me to buy it, take it home,
even though the poems themselves are already on my shelves
    but not like this
and besides, who wouldn't take a little more
of O'Hara's insouciance, his seemingly careless brilliance,
to help them through the day?
    See?
The rain has stopped, the cat is outside,
studiously ignoring the blackbird
digging its orange beak into the earth
at the far end of the garden,
and, picking up the book of poems, I consign Berg
to another day
and set off in search of my coat and shoes.
    Let's go!

Last Days of August

Last days of August:
the blackberry bushes heavy with fruit
that has come late this summer,
dark and bulbous
squishy to the touch.

Between the little bouts of nausea
that catch in her throat and then recede,
she has been reading the book of poems
he gave her before leaving –
The Half-Finished Heaven: Tomas Transtromer –
the painting by Vermeer,
Woman in Blue Reading a Letter,
reproduced on the cover.

> *empty houses*
> *feeling their way forward in the falling snow*

The words cast her adrift,
the child inside her
turning on the tide.

There had been words between them earlier:
sharp, resentful, blurred by anger,
his kiss cold and quick
on the clamminess of her skin;
she feels bloated, helpless.

> *The letter she has had seven days now*
> *seven days since his going*

> *The paper bears the marks of her hands*
> *fingers rich with oil from the lamp*

that spilt a little as she turned up the wick;
the blue jet of flame that matches, almost,
the smock she is wearing

He is coming back: he is not coming back.
The words spin away from her like stars

Behind her the contours of Terra Incognita
hang loose upon the eggshell wall –
a land of other lakes unvisited,
fields and trees

Beside her the table where he ate
the book he read
the blue chair on which he sat

When the child kicks and stirs
she presses a hand against her swollen belly
searches in vain
for a cold place in her heart

From another room, a clock
striking the hour; outside,
the sounds of traffic slowing,
quickening, changing gear,
people leaving, going about
their business, returning.

She has a hospital appointment
that afternoon at three, a friend
calling at four for tea.

Time enough to fold
the blackberries into a sponge
and allow it to cool.

The book slides from her fingers
to the floor. *All my love,*
on the fly leaf, the month and his name.

  What is written cannot be taken back

When she stoops to pick it up
the child kicks inside her
a reminder, an anchor
holding her to the day
and everyday ...

August, September ...

Winter Notebook
for Robert Hass

My daughter, the youngest, has a date tonight,
the Odeon, a quarter to eight. A first date, too.
Great Expectations. No pressure there, then.
A last glance in the mirror and she's gone.
I remember the movie, the original not the remake,
the gasp, the tightening at the back of the neck
when the convict rises up from the marsh,
so that, running away, the boy runs smack into him –
not knowing that sometimes the thing you're running from
is in the very place you're running to
– only life can teach you that –
I hope the one she's with is kind, her fragile heart
too full of yet ungiven love to break.

Earlier today, the sun strong but low in the sky,
I walked with friends a slow ten miles across open country,
mostly arable land, skirting the edges of villages,
small farms, a stand of oak; mud clinging to our boots
as we descend the last low hill towards home,
beech trees decanting light into the flat water of the canal.
And, for a moment, I think of Constable,
what he'd have made of this scene,
and of my grandfather, my mother's father,
a weekend painter, the grandfather I never met,
mercurial, absent, always on the move
from theatre to small theatre, lodgings in Lambeth
or Brixton, Brighton, Stoke-on-Trent;
little time to look after a daughter,
pay heed to her needs the way a father should;
my mother still talking with pride,
in the nursing home where she ended her days,
of the book she was awarded as a prize,

the one time they stayed long enough in one place
for her to complete a whole term of school.

My father's father was the opposite, silent, unspeaking,
small pan of Camp coffee, black as pitch,
forever simmering on the kitchen stove.
Later, when I came to Dickens, he was the perfect Magwitch,
escaped from the prison ships on the estuary
to haunt my dreams. Still at primary school,
I used to go to their house on my way home,
sit in their small kitchen with bread and jam and read,
listening for my grandfather's step upon the stair:
one day when I was certain I was alone,
something made me turn towards the doorway and he was there:
'Have you been taking money from Nanny's purse?'
His voice like the voice of God. 'No,' I said. 'No, I promise.'
'Don't ever let me catch you doing that again.'
I never did.

Years later, when she was old and living on her own,
my grandfather dead, she fell, my nan, struck her head
on the edge of the hearth and lay there till her hair
caught fire. When finally they found her, unconscious,
she was badly burned, and although the doctors
did what they could, along with her hair and half her face,
her mind had gone. They took her to the asylum at Colney
Hatch, the looney bin – no circumvention in those days –
if you were mad you were mad – and there she died.

Now the thinking has all changed: we are welcomed
both at birth and death, our presence a given.
At my youngest daughter's birth, I looked on,
amazed at how she slipped so bloodily into life,
breeching the waters in a gasp for air, her lungs,
even then, before the midwive's slap, all too ready to protest.

'You know, I do like you quite a lot', she said
the other day, 'about 80% of the time, even though
the rest of the time you drive me mad'.

My friend, Tony, with whom I first listened,
really listened to jazz, the two of us practising
in his parents' bedroom, he on saxophone,
me drums, rustling brushes in four-four time
across the top of an old suitcase –
my friend Tony is in a hospice:
the volunteers at the desk welcoming and polite,
all chemo stopped, the carpet deep, the furnishings
not too bright; visiting, we keep our voices low,
talk around you, and just when we think
you've drifted off to sleep, you rebuke us
for some mistaken reference to a recording
you know well, Brubeck, perhaps, Mulligan or Getz;
and when Jim retells a joke you first told him
many years before – it's punchline too crude
to be repeated here – how marvellous to see
you throw back your head and laugh out loud.

For now I sit alone with you and watch you sleep,
breath like brittle plastic breaking inside your chest,
and, for a moment, without feeling I have the right,
I reach out and hold your hand.

One day soon I will push through the doors,
present myself at the desk, only to hear the news
we know must come. It happens, no matter
what expectations we have, fulfilled or not.
And not dramatically, like some monster
rising from the marsh to seize us, drag us down,
but deftly, quietly, like someone switching out the light.

There ... you're gone.

Ghosts of a Chance

Evenings on Seventy-Third Street

Soft rock of traffic steadying down,
four pieces of chicken, fried potato chips,
dill pickles – ridged and thick as fingers –
coleslaw, Coke. Despite our best efforts
by the time we walk it home, circles
of grease, dark through the paper sack,
have stained your clothes and mine,
a smear across the silk blouse you bought
for best, below the spots where coffee
dribbled from your mug two nights before,
watching the news on tv.

While you snap the lock shut, slide
the bolt across, I am sharing food
onto paper plates; your book open,
face down where you left it,
pad on which I'm writing
is on the floor by my chair.
The radio, which we left playing,
chances its arm at a contemporary
string quartet and I sense you will
rise soon, licking your fingers
free from chicken, wiping them,
to be certain, down your skirt,
before lifting Lee Wiley from the record rack –
the Liberty Music Shop recordings 39-40 –
singing songs of love, but not for me.

An hour now since either of us has spoken,
felt the need to speak.

Till it Shines

We danced together.
Oh, yes, we did.
That evening and after.
Stepped around each other,
pleased, cautious,
prepared to be impressed.

Out on the street, along the canal,
your hand moved like light
against the smoothness of my skin.
We could be so happy together
you said; brought your bone china
cups and placed them on my shelf.

Look into my eyes, you said.
Look into my eyes.

Out there at the tide line,
arms wound so close
they could be dancing,
but no, they are standing,
this couple, perfectly still,
and anyone looking at them
can see how much they are in love.

All that was in another country.
Another time.
We were different people
and resemblances, like memories,
are blurred.

While I pored over colour cards
choosing paint,
you knew already you were leaving me
just not when

Somewhere between the terracotta
And the midnight blue
I heard you clear your throat

Look into my eyes, you said.
Look into my eyes ...

Hollywood Canteen

It seems too much of a cliché,
almost, to tell it, but there,
up on the counter
of the Hollywood Canteen,
there among the images
of Marilyn, James Dean,
she pushes back her plate,
lights her cigarette
and right over the juke box
she says, nineteen:

> I hate films that end like that,
> stuck out on the porch
> in the middle of nowhere
> watching the sun go down –
> as though it could ever happen.
> Jesus! It's like your parents
> bringing you up to believe
> it's possible to tell the truth
> out there, when one minute
> after they let you out into the world,
> you can see everyone else is lying.
> I mean, you just try being nice out there,
> just try it! You won't last five minutes
> and I'll tell you this, I haven't met
> a single person since I was sixteen
> who wasn't a bitch underneath
> and I haven't got the strength
> to stand up to them, not on my own,
> and that's what I am.
> And happiness, that's a laugh
> and one thing I am sure of,
> it isn't sitting out on a dumb porch

in the middle of Iowa, staring
into some technicolour sunset.

She turned her head aside
and closed her eyes
and when she did that
she was as beautiful
as I had ever seen her.

What do you think, she said,
the pancakes with the maple syrup?
You think we should have the ice cream
as well? Maybe the chocolate sauce?

Seeing my face, she smiled.

Remember?

It was snowing in New York but that was Easter:
we walked past the rink where Clayburgh skated
in *An Unmarried Woman*, ate hot pretzels
and stood on line for pasta and clam sauce.

(can you still taste that?)

I can't recall what I wanted for dessert
except the waiter said, "That's disgusting!"
and refused to take my order.

Later we cruised the Village, hands
punched down in our pockets,
Kevin and I browsing the schedules
at the Bleecker Street Cinema
while you went next door into
the Magic Shoe Store and bought
a pair of bright scarlet boots

with wings

remember?

yes (you say) oh, yes

Between

Labour Day and Thanksgiving,
Christmas and New Year's;
between waking
and first light;
between the sharp cotton sheets
in the attic where she sleeps;
between lifting her cup
from its saucer
and setting it back down

she thinks of him
less and less often.

Hemlock

It keeps coming back to this:
we're sitting outside a restaurant,
on a terrace or beneath a canopy
alongside this quiet street –
Berlin, perhaps. Paris. Budapest.
Vienna was brighter,
we liked the way the waiters
disappeared for hours
leaving us to our notebooks,
papers, coffee growing cold.
You slipped a sweater round
your shoulders, pale moths
flirting with the light,
and there, between the fish
and the olives, salad thick
with fennel, offered me
so much of my life I had wanted
almost, it seemed, on a plate.

In the hotel I punched the bathroom wall,
screamed till both our voices bled;
so frightened what you were giving
I might really take.

This far along and still it cradles us,
indistinct beneath our conversations,
the scent of aniseed, clinging unbidden
to our fingers and our tongues.

Goodnight, Fuzzy Stone
"Orphans are notorious for interior games"
John Irving – *The Cider House Rules*

Inside the folds of his box Fuzzy Stone has a dream:
when he picks up the phone she says she will be home
from work a little late; when she arrives
there are flowers in her arms, so many flowers.
They sit at either end of the sofa while she tells
him of her day; they have not yet kissed –
he has learned not to claim too much too soon.

He believes in Santa Claus, the tooth fairy,
the power of love, the end of the rainbow.
Believes if he picks up the phone it will be her: always.

When he was four his mother packed him off
with his own fork and spoon to find the party.

> "Fuzzy is a loveable child who would benefit
> from a warm and caring family, preferably one
> with brothers and sisters of a similar age."

Slowly fingering the lines, mouth moving
to the words, Fuzzy recognises himself and smiles.

Cars come slowly over the hill,
even in the worst of winter there are cars,
singly or in convoy, and when they leave
another face than his own stares back
at Fuzzy through a blur of glass.

When he was sixteen they gave him
a new pair of second-hand shoes,
a travel warrant and a testimonial:

"Fuzzy is a pleasant enough young man,
decent and fundamentally honest,
but when things become too stressful
he likes to climb back inside his box."

In the bus station he sleeps with one ear open
beside the bank of telephones.
There are other places: the launderette,
the air ducts out at the bakery,
or his favourite, behind the curtains
in the camera booth – colour photos
three for a pound – he loves to watch
them slip into sight, always when
you had given up hoping, there!
Like magic. Like dreams.

The phone rings and he picks it up:
climbs back inside his box.

What he really wants to do is drive
the wet miles till she holds him tight
and whispers (as he is certain she would)
"Turn over and let me snuggle you up."
Isn't that the kind of thing lovers say?

Say good night, Fuzzy Stone.

Grace Notes

Let's say it's one of those
insubstantial inner-city days,
from the flower beds in the park
to the slim-hipped cellist
playing the inevitable Bach.

And say, strolling home, I chance to pass
this bar just hours after David Murray
has jet-lagged in from New York.
It's light enough still for the doors
to be open out onto the street;
the sound and the small crowd
draw me inside, and there on stage
before bass and drums he stands:
back arched, chest pigeoned forward,
horn angled outwards as he rocks
lightly back from heel to toe,
toeing the line of a calypso so true,
the crowd, as one, leans back and smiles,
relaxed, not noticing those heels
have lifted with an extra bounce
and before anyone can blink
his left leg kicks out in the curve
of a high hurdler; his tenor twists
and soars and lifts us, holds us to him,
wrapped in curlicues of sound,
blessed by the effortless grace
of his playing.

Finished, he steps off stage
and I don't know what to do
with this silence – except from nowhere
I am thinking of you, your mouth,

the hazel switch of colour in your eyes,
the way you stand a little to one side
and cock your head and stare;
swell of your belly warm against my face,
your breasts, your smile ...

God! You are beautiful!

Miracle Man

Rain is everywhere.
The barn awash at its moorings,
an army of pine borers drills the loft walls
where I sway and sail the night.

Come morning, the rain gauge is full,
five inches in thirty hours.
Husks of pumpkin flop across the garden,
like a tangle of orange buoys.
Lost, the dogs paddle out and back.
Wings glistening like heavy plastic,
a blue jay skids startled off the woodshed roof.

We crowd the kitchen with excitement:
six a.m. and the vain promise of early light.
And because it's what we've learned
we hold our breath against the ghosts of rainbows
hung along the soughing of the wind.
Do nothing till there's nothing left to do.

Unceasing, it falls three days more,
sweeping in from the ocean, a moving wall
of water stripping trees along the north-east shore.
The road to the island is washed away;
the car caught by its axles and held fast.
Food is rationed; each trip to well
or outhouse measured in need.

This is the stuff to sluice away
romance and miracles, caught like seeds
in a swirl of topsoil and flushed
along the channels of the field,
clean to the clamflats of the bay.

Sunsets

"Grandad looks like John Wayne,"
my daughter said, pirouetting away.

In the westerns I wrote he filled in corners –
the stage coach driver, the friendly sheriff
with spreading paunch and bowed back,
his gun never drawn in anger,
yet stubborn as a mule when the chips are down.

In photographs he holds me high above
his head like a talisman: pride bright
in his blue eyes I could never fulfil.

Writing, he stands between my sentences:
bits of a life that catch like grit in the mouth.
Once I ran, sobbing, after him until, reaching
down, he swung me, safe, in his arms.

He stands in all the doorways of my childhood.
Stands for my meanness, my grudging thanks,
those shifts of direction which push him
further and further behind.
Driving home to visit I'd passed him
on the road before I realised, stooped
and suddenly slow, one leg turned sideways,
an old man I'd failed to recognise.

Laughter and meaning clogged thick in his lungs:
they moved him to a private room and fitted
a green mask fast over his face; each breath
rattled dry stones along the bed of his throat,
his mouth peeled back and back
until it disappeared.

Yet a week or so before he died,
the old smile alive for a moment in his eyes,
he beckoned the prettiest nurse and as
she bent to catch his words,
nuzzled the hard plastic of his mask
against her face to steal a kiss:
an act of imagination great
as any John Wayne ever made.

She Explains It Another Way
for Lee Harwood

As if horsemen appeared
nudging the edges of the frame

Dust across the sun
& the way their clothes
stuck to them as they came
towards the house

We would leave after a meal
carefully prepared   glazed ham
pitchers of water misting the glass

The stranger stands a way off
smoking a cigarette

The slight squeak of the rocker
stills on the porch out of sight

My father's words, not quite
looking at me as he spoke

He is a fair man
you will see ...

   She explains it another way:

   When my mother was nine years old
   she got off the train at Colchester station
   a hand at her back
   moving her across the platform
   to where a man was waiting

A man seen through steam
(I suppose there was steam)
smoking a cigarette

"You're going to live with your father now"

He stepped hesitant towards her

(I hope he was hesitant)

He is a fair man
you will see ...

As if horsemen appeared
slow across the centre of the frame

We rode for three days
through country that refused
to dip or fall   hills in a smoke
of cloud to the west
interchangeable

Owning it, he smiled

He performed his duties
handsomely   politely
nicotine on his hands

The house square behind its arch
not a little impressive
and between the outbuildings
the scurry for his return

Smoke from the chimney
(there was smoke)
caught

against the patina of sky

He helps me down

(He is a fair man you will see...)

An End of Wishing

Like a character in an Ida Lupino movie
she had all the moves:
base line to main line in three short years.

So much hangs on the outswing
of her serve;
red bandanna, blue of her shirt
beaten black with sweat

On a cold night in England,
as her opponent waits,
she lifts her head away from the trees,
foot-faulting in someone else's shoes
imagining other places
other names she might choose

"It's bad when you're sixteen,
but when you're forty, it's no better."

The only thing is to keep the ball in play
and when the chance comes
smash it hard as you can

Hard, fast and beautiful.

Temps Greatest Hits Vol II

"Are you in love? Is it going badly?"
"I'm always in love, sooner or later it goes badly."
Bernard Malamud – *Dubin's Lives*
for David Kresh

I wake at two to the sound of your breathing,
slowly realise the sea has fooled me once more
shuffling back along the upgang shore

I get up and don't switch on the light:
a tideswell like moving bone

Like Monk fingering *These Foolish Things*
from broken glass

Like train times ticking down

This place smells of flowers
and I think it smells of you
but of course it doesn't

Up here at night poems bloom like dark

Last winter in Amsterdam
applecake fumbling from our fingers
we chased the cold from canal to canal,
afternoon movies, the American Bar,
it seemed nothing but games and glances,
foolish chances

The moment before it happened
I was looking the other way –
the perfect writer's pose.

This is no 'apples' nor even 'sea'
though both are mentioned;
this is not an exercise,
a way of sealing 'difference'

What hurts isn't the thought
of you lying in this bed/that bed
his bed/her bed, loving/being loved

What hurts is the image I've never seen:
you are with a new lover
hand in hand down from the city
walking that walk
and
    oh, baby
        I ain't too proud to beg
           ain't too proud to plead

Oklahoma Territory

Four or five times Jug lets the bottle fall
from his fingers, till finally it bounces
down between the trombones,
Russell opening one eye mid-solo
to see a fifth of Johnny Walker slide to a rest,
buffing the shine of his patent shoe.

And later, the dance hall owner, who doubles
as Baptist minister, starts in on intoxication
and immorality, drunkenness and wantonness and
ends up withholding ten per cent of the band's take.

Russell takes it anyway, philosophically,
fines Jug a night's wages and lays out the last
of several last warnings. Back on the bus,
those not already sleeping, talk in stage whispers
of offers from Bill McKinney, Fletcher Henderson,
Jean Goldkette. When the banjo player
deals himself a pair of eights from the bottom of the deck
somewhere south of Oklahoma City,
no-one's got the energy to complain.

It goes on like that, more or less,
for ten or twelve days ...

The marquee out front of the Wasita Theatre
in Elk City advertises Tom Mix in *King Cowboy*
and off to one side, *Russell Grant and His
Midwest Rhythm Kings: One Night Only.*

We're playing for dancing after the movie.
Which is when the girl comes up to us, Russell
and myself, not a girl at all, a woman, black hair

flecked with white, skin that can only come from
the reservation, boiled bones and plain dirt every
day of her life. She wants to sing with the band.

Sweet Georgia Brown comes in too fast,
falls apart too soon, and she's left standing there,
staring down at chicken feet wedged into borrowed shoes.

Russell speaks to her quietly, calls Jug front
and centre, sixteen bars of muted trumpet,
I Can't Give You Anything ...
This time the tempo's right, the crowd is quiet,
– something about the voice –
and when she steps back from the mike,
brass bass supple behind me,
I play the best thirty-two bars of sax
I ever played before or since.

Turns out she's got kids, a cabinful of cats
and scrawny dogs, an old man doing
five to ten upstate, a father going blind:
she'll ditch them all to join us on the road,
eleven men and a book of hand-me-down
arrangements, stalking our own sweat
ten months out of every twelve.

Russell shakes his head; he doesn't put her down,
he's kind. A bunch of the boys and myself argue
him into a corner but there's no changing his mind.
He knows what it'd be like, one woman on the bus,
knows he's got trouble enough already.

After that, pretty soon
it all starts to fall apart.

Two dates cancel out in Kansas;
Jug gets a telegram to join the Orange Blossoms Band
at the Greystone Ballroom in Detroit.
At a stop-off on 44, someone breaks into the bus,
steals a tuba and the pants to our dress suits.
The rest of the saxophone section are last seen
thumbing a ride east.

I bum the price of hash and eggs from Russell
and leave him in the back booth dealing solitaire.
I went with him when I was but nineteen
and now I'm twenty-one and the last thing
I want to see is the look on my father's face
when I walk back through his front door.

Outside I take a smoke, and already
there are more stars than I could hope to count.
In not so many hours, my brothers will start
putting on their work clothes for another day.
And I can stand here, staring out, and waiting
for the light, and all there'll ever be around me,
whichever way I turn,
will be just another shade of corn.

Clearing

Back at the hotel,
a small, family-run affair
close to all amenities,
a reputation for hospitality
and local specialities,
they think about a shower
but slump instead
on single beds
placed head to head.
Whatever the tour guide had said
was inadvertantly missing
from the phrase book,
and when finally they'd arrived,
the Palace of Culture
had been locked and barred.
She thinks for a moment
of removing her dress,
touching his mouth to her breast,
but it is too hot, too cold,
too liable not to succeed.
She opens her book
and starts to read.
The mist that has lain
across the airport since
they arrived
shows little sign of clearing.

Mutton

Just a bunch of hippy kids & bleeding hearts,
travelling across America by Audabon bus,
picking up credits in life sciences and why
the disadvantaged live close to the land.

Still the dog ran off the reservation after them,
out across the desert in a hundred yards of yelping,
one-fifty, more, till they pulled over and took him in,
brought him out here to Maine, 70 acres and a cabin,
two square meals a day. Not too much traffic
up the track from Crow Neck Road,
still, time to time, he'll take out after a car
or slow-departing truck, but at the bend
he'll stop & turn & head back home.

Without reason he'll stand afternoons between
the amber punctured pumpkins & the barn,
stare off into the distance, barking for an hour
at no more than the sound of his own voice.

But most of all he loves to slow walk under
the gaze of herons down into the edges of the ocean
& lay his belly in the fastness of grey mud;
to sit on rock & stare out at clam fishers
and yellow-legged waders, at what to him is still
a mystery: the sloping islands, the vastness of the sea.

Ghost of a Chance

He plays the tune lazily,
pretty much the way he must
have heard Billie sing it,
but slower, thick-toned,
leaning back on the beat,
his mind half on the melody,
half on the gin.

Between takes he stands,
head down, shrunken inside
a suit already overlarge,
cheeks sunken in.
He thinks of her, Billie:
already it is possible
he has started to bleed within.

From the control room, laughter,
but that's not the sound he hears;
tenor closer to his mouth,
he turns towards the doors:
unseen, not quite unbidden,
someone has just slipped in.

At the end of eight bars
he closes his eyes and blows.
After two choruses he will cover
his mouthpiece with his shield:
not play again.

Blue Territory

Impossible to tell
why I keep coming back to this:
the blue that clusters high to one corner
   the boxiness
almost neatness of it.
Landscape of colour
fields spread wide,
stones stacked high,
two boulders, orange brown,
with slates on top.

Such warmth.
Your hands.
O'Hara's 'Poem Read at Joan Mitchell's'.
Women walking past with flowers,
orange and blue in constant flow,
thin lines of paint running down
   like gold
   like fireflies
   like dust of wheat
     spread by the wind.

Like the hair of the girl at the table opposite,
falling long past her shoulders,
but I'm still thinking of you
and wondering should I take
this copy of *Lunch Poems* from my bag
   and browse
or sit a little longer
toying with my walnut cake
   and thinking
I'd rather be sipping
a late evening espresso

at Bar Italia
and later wandering across the street
      to Ronnie's
to catch Spike's second set
      or Stan's
or even just be home with you
listening to Lester and Teddy Wilson
play 'These Foolish Things' ...

that first time I walked into Patrick's flat
and Lester was on the stereo playing clarinet

... but I stay here just a little longer
long enough for the girl with long hair
to take her leave and then, still thinking of you,
for this almost perfect painting
to reinvent itself against this pane of glass
      and I know
how something in my blood would sing
      if you walked in
the way white light breathes through canvas
      surfacing the blue.

Bluer Than This

What Would You Say?

What would you say of a man who can play
three instruments at once – saxophone,
manzello and stritch – but who can neither
tie his shoelace nor button his fly?

Who stumbles through basements,
fumbles open lacquered boxes,
a child's set of drawers,
strews their contents across bare boards –
seeds, vestments, rabbit paws?

Whose favourite words are vertiginous,
gourd, dilate? Whose fantasy is snow?
Who can trace in the dirt the articular process
of the spine, the pulmonary action of the heart?

Would you say he was blind?

Would you say he was missing you?

You Did It! You Did It!

It was Roland Kirk, wasn't it?
Who played all those instruments?
I saw him. St. Pancras Town Hall.
Nineteen sixty four.

The same year, at the old Marquee,
I saw Henry 'Red' Allen,
face swollen like sad fruit,
sing I've Got the World on a String'
in a high almost falsetto moan.

Rahassan Roland Kirk,
on stage in this cold country,
cramming his mouth with saxophones,
harmonica, reed trumpet, piccolo and clarinet,
exultant, black and blind.

      'You did it! You did it!
      You did it! You did it!

Daring us to turn our backs,
stop our ears, our hearts,
deny the blood wherever it leads us:
the whoop and siren call
of flutes and whistles,
spiralling music, unconfined.

Talking About Cities

Horses, she tells him, if I'm late
there are these marvellous pictures of horses.

What he looks at, crouched low,
face close against the glass, are still lives:
mottled eggs and feathers, pebbles, nests of grass.

During the war he used to sit
cross-legged with wonder and wait
for the first chicks to wobble and wave
their stubby wings and run across
his outstretched hands.

When he tells her this she dismisses it for what it is:
another sly metaphor for fatherhood.
It's the horses she loves,
the way their necks strain hard against the frame,
their wild beauty, uncontained.

Outside, though, walking on the embankment
in the sun, so many sets of twins
they're difficult to ignore,
and when the clarinetist – really, this is true –
begins 'I Thought About You',
she springs sideways to straddle the wall,
and he dares to place his fingers
one by one, warm and safe
inside the nest of her hands
and this is every city
they have ever seen or will ever see.

Chet Baker

looks out from his hotel room
across the Amstel to the girl
cycling by the canal who lifts
her hand and waves and when
she smiles he is back in times
when every Hollywood producer
wanted to turn his life
into that bitter-sweet story
where he falls badly, but only
in love with Pier Angeli,
Carol Lynley, Natalie Wood;
that day he strolled into the studio,
fall of fifty-two, and played
those perfect lines across
the chords of *My Funny Valentine*,
and now, when he looks up from
his window and her passing smile
into the blue of a perfect sky,
he knows this is one of those
rare days when he can truly fly.

Driven by Rain

And when finally I look up, lost,
from this book, I'm shocked
by the sudden wash of rain that blows
in swathes along this slow suburban
street I'm trying to call home.

So strange, the way it can be there from nowhere,
filling out your world, everything you see: memory.

That day we climbed almost to the summit of Cadillac,
so hot you went skinny-dipping in the lake
while I sat propped against hard rock,
drank from our thermos and read,
only stopping when you emerged, glistening,
eager to make the most of our time ...
And then, when we clambered, exhausted,
over the last broad grey stones,
the sky, from nowhere, black with thunder,
those first stabs of lightning fixing the peaks
opposite and closer by the second, so that,
yards only short of the summit, we turned
and ran, laughing with panic, leaping over rocks,
newly wet and slippery with rain, never losing
our footing, me clinging to your hand as if
my life depended on it, which, of course, it did.

Slow

for Lee Harwood
& in memory of Paul Evans, 1945-1991

It was all right until the slow lurch towards
Battersea – the Power Station in decay – that new
building you always pointed out as we went past ...

A small stone loosed into the valley like memory,
so far you cannot hear it fall.
All day I've kept this at bay.

Walking with Lee along the front by the sea,
ruins of the old West Pier, shift and change
of housefronts between Brighton and Hove.
Small cups of coffee, thick and black; we go out
for focaccia and cheese and bring them back.

Photos of Paul Evans in Lee's room, child in his arms.
Two years I sat in his classes as soft-spoken
he opened out poetry before me

   "Here ... read/
      listen to this"

He was dead instantly, it said.

So trivial
    anything I fear or feel compared to this

The way when we cross the river your heart leaped.

   "Remember walking back to our cabin in the valley
   in Maine? None of this is gone from my memory, though
   thinking about it makes me weep."

At the station Lee and I shake hands,
spurred on by talk of poetry and poets, Dada & the Surreal,
the kids who live with him alternately through the week.

I board my train so far from death and you:
alone in the compartment read memories of Paul,
friends, daughters, wives. Signals shuttle us
from side to side.

      The river.

For one more moment I am here with you

      ("You move me ... and the thought of you")

The walk I will never take, child in my arms, slow
to where you have set up your cameras down by the bay.

Out of Silence
Squaw Valley, 1995

How the light diffuses round house corners;
redwood walls, the breaking colour of packed earth,
ochre in the mouth.

The red woodpecker testilly chiselling sap from a small ash
the only sound in the valley.

Lilac

5 or 6 and drying me from the bath,
warm before the fire, my father said,
a glance over his shoulder, we'll have
to stop this soon, in front of your mother,
you're getting to be a big boy now.

And so I entered those years of ignorance
and shame, doors quickly closed and clothes
pulled down, the Sunday paper cancelled,
the book of drawings my uncle had
exchanged for his leg in France
no longer in the wardrobe drawer,
those packets wrapped in newspaper
and stuffed into the dustbin rusted through
with blood – all disappeared from sight.

Though I remember once, playing table tennis
with my mother, mesmerised as she bent low
to scoop the ball over the net,
the way her breasts swung loose beneath
the thin brown cotton of her top
and me flushed there, struggling to ignore
even as I strained to see, I suppose
I was 10 or 12 by then and old enough
to wonder what a breast might be.

I did not think of this for years, mother,
for there were girls, I found, less careful
with their bodies, women too, until that
Christmas, my father dead and scattered
to the ground, when you released yourself
from hospital so we might spend together
that last festive time and I carried you

from bed to chair and chair to bed,
lifted you onto the toilet and pulled up
your dress, eased down your pants,
bones unfussed by flesh
that crumbled, a little more each time,
like chalk against my hands.
We did this unspeaking, unashamed,
the slow washing of pain
as I ran the flannel across your ribs,
the shadows of breasts that hung
like bruised lilac against your chest.

Self Portrait
Bonnard at Le Cannet

Cold here, this room you sit in, 1945;
your corner table, vase of flowers and white cloth,
grey scarf close about your neck.
You sit and smoke, patient for cognac
warm in its glass; a white cup with gold rim,
the small black coffee she will bring.

Again and again sketched in his diary –
Saturday, February 26th; Tuesday the 15th of June –
like an otter she would ease, sleek, into the bath,
snug against the curve of porcelain.

On the radio, news of the Armistice,
a hastily articulated peace, the Jews.
The air is rimed with smoke, far echo of guns.
The small electric heater stands unplugged,
no fire in the grate.

Marthe – why does she not come?

These last mornings you have walked
between the almond and the olive trees,
gazed over red roofs toward the fullness of the sea.
You painted ochres, oranges and browns,
cupboards steeped in jars and bottles,
herbs in bunches, greengages and plums,
golden apples, persimmons.

In the studio the slow shunt of trucks,
smell of paint thick on your hands;
stiff-legged before the mirror
you blow warmth into your fingers.

Head shaved, ready, this is not so difficult,
one portrait, all that's left.

A gash of colour for the mouth,
those veins, blue, drawn down
across the fabric of the face;
black hollows where the eyes would have been,
burnt out by bodies that lay ripening,
close-pressed between trees, their richness
leaking back into the soil, beyond reach of seeing,
stripped beneath the surface of the sea.

Interior with Roses

Morning. When I fetch the paper a little after six
the pavements are ridged with ice.
In a downstairs room across the street
a man sits under an orange light;
he is writing a troublesome letter
explaining why he and his wife are separating.
Why is she leaving him? How best to express this?
He reaches out and turns down the lamp.

We went by train to Sheffield to see the Vuillard;
the gallery seemed impossible to find.
Except for one room, the paintings were cramped
and badly hung, the only ones which might
have lifted our hearts we had already seen.
Patches of red askew at the edges of beds,
a shirt thrown carelessly across a leather chair,
his mother sweeping out the room, moss roses
straining for the sun – a few more days
and they'll be strewn across the dark wood floor –
the door open so she can hear him cross
to the window where he switches on the lamp;
the scratch of nib on paper as he writes.
The orange hue that runs through everything.

The house where we first lived together,
geraniums in boxes at the windows,
the orange patio where we'd sit with fruit
bought from the Chinese brothers in the market –
oranges, peaches, plums – juice bright on our mouths
and hands; the table where sometimes I sat and wrote.

The man across the street has finished or just given up,
his wife has called him to the table, mushroom-barley soup;

71

a dash of red beneath the orange cloth;
the room spotless, swept, the roses on the dresser
already leaning; in a day or two, maybe tomorrow,
their petals will begin to fall.

The broom stands in the corner and the shirt
has been folded neatly in the drawer.
When I walked home to where you waited,
winter roses framed by London brick,
fresh smell of coffee, music streaming out,
all I had to do, step to the open window,
call your name, walk in.

Failed Sonnet Home

The windowboxes outside the Clocktower Café
are delerious with bloom. Cappuccino with
chocolate and cinnamon. Blueberry muffin.
How many more days can the sky sustain
this absurdity of blue? I can taste vanilla
from the pines. And you. You know the other day
Jake drove me to Truckee in his van
and in Safeway I was stalled mid-aisle
by the scent of that hot-buttered toast
we shared before you drove me to the train.
How far we are away! Crimson columbine,
black centre of violet pansy, its yellow eye –
one thing you learn here: how little soil
it takes to nourish the most stubborn root.

North Coast

Once, we stayed here, out of season,
arcades and the Magpie Café closed,
clouds massed like bulkheads in the northern sky
and around the municipal grandstand
only the melismatic cry of gulls.
Close by our feet, winter lay coiled like rope.
At night, hope hung across the water like a child.
What is never shared, can never be lost.

When she was seven or eight
I brought my daughter here to stay.
Her first time in an old-fashioned B & B,
hot water bottles and flasks of coffee on request.
She laid out her clothes, folded and neat,
each item in its proper drawer,
alarm clock wound and set for seven,
books and diary on the square oak table
nudged against the bed.

There have been other lovers, other nights.
The town, I heard this morning, is falling
rock by rock and day by day into the sea.
Tied up against each forecast,
fishing boats, all colours, rack and slide.
My daughter rang me yesterday from France,
she and the man she's lived with for years
are breaking up. I shall come here again, yes,
I think so, with someone else or on my own.
We cling to what we can, and the rest,
one way or another, clings to us.

Couples

1. Edward Hopper: "Room in New York", 1932

With one finger she picks out the tune
the way her mother showed her,
slow afternoons when the dogs lay aside
their indifferent barking and moths
hung sleeping from the inside of the blinds;
distant rattle of ice inside her mother's glass
and whatever burned inside her
cold water and calamine could not touch.
In the close air of the apartment she has been
thinking more and more of those times.
The newspaper rustles behind her, whatever
her husband is reading commands his attention.
Although he has loosened neither
waistcoat nor tie, the yellow distemper
of the walls has begun to sweat.
The red dress she is wearing
has a bow bunched high at its back,
like a flower that once, petal by petal,
he would have reached out and unfastened
before her mirrored eyes.
His shirt so white that to turn and look
at it would be to be blinded by the moon.

2. Edward Hopper: "Excursion into Philosophy", 1959

He has been reading the *Tractatus*, Wittgenstein,
the footnotes make him laugh; the book open
on the bed, the blue divan. How to explain
the duality of grief and joy, relief and guilt.
The way her breathing, as she lies behind him,
legs drawn up, exposed, her back
not quite touching his, touches his heart.
They have been together fifteen years
and he believes that is enough.
The sun burns low along the ripening wheat
that looks like the wheat in the painting by Van Gogh,
the postcard she bought him that day in Portland, Maine,
and told him if he ever left her she would truly die.
He picks up his book and begins again to read,
but sets it back down, drawn to the window by the sun,
the sound of a meadow lark in the field.
The only signs in the morning they were there
will be her red hair, snagged at one corner
of the pillow; the slight impression, fading,
on the mattress where they lay.

Apples

My father is dying.
Scent of apples from the night stand.
I reach out my hand and rest one
hard against my face; he taught me
to tell the real thing from the fake:
hold it close beside the ear and shake.
A genuine Cox, the seeds will rattle
loose inside their case.
You see. He told me
and I swallowed every word by rote.
Five cotton towns of Lancashire,
five woollen towns, four rivers
that flow into the Wash – Witham,
Welland, Nen and Great Ouse.
Once learned, never forgotten.

My father is dying.
He died nine years ago this June.
They phoned from the hospital with the news.
His face a cask once used
for storing living things.
A cup of tea, grown cold and orange,
on the stand beside the bed.
Fingernails like horn, unclipped.
Though dead, my father is still dying.
Oh, slowly, sure and slow as the long fall of rain.
I reach out again for the apple
and bite into its flesh and hold him,
bright and sharp,
safe inside the hollow of my mouth.

Charlie Parker in Green Shoes

Back in the City, I walk south on Seventh,
cut across Broadway, joust with the traffic
round Times Square; finally hit 42nd Street
around 6th Avenue. From the squeak
of the subway doors as the train sways
the tracks crosstown, to the buskers
in Bryant Park, hustling out-of-towners
on their way back from brunch,
music pumps beneath your feet.
Ornithology, Dizzy Atmosphere, Constellation,
Groovin' High – Bird, who died at thirty-five,
each year called to do the work of two,
but still that's not enough.
"Bird Lives!" tagged on the walls,
the scrape of chalk and spray of paint
seguing into his last breath.

No heaven's hip enough to hold him!
Out on remission, he scores from a dude
on roller skates in Washington Square,
picks up a fifth of Seagrams and hits
the Magic Shoe Store where he buys –
wait for it! – green shoes.

He remembers his first record date,
thirty dollars, union scale; Dean Benedetti
following him everywhere, pockets overflowing
with wire spools, magnetic tape, keyhole saw,
the slender lead and microphone
recording every note he ever played.
He remembers the first night at the club
Chan Richardson walked in;
high heels, high colour, black hair.

Tastes Chinese dinners, barbecued ribs,
sandwiches, custom built, three layers
of smoked fish, Chicago corned beef,
green tomatoes, kosher pickles, coleslaw.
A snack. Smack. Scuffling bills from friends
and strangers in the men's room and out
along the street. He feels the wind
that whipped his head as he roamed the city,
rode the subway, Battery Park to Harlem,
Brooklyn into Queens; he sold his horn
a hundred times, his heart but not his soul.
Cirrhosis of the liver, stomach ulcers,
pneumonia – he would do it all again.

Horn out of hock he heads for 52nd Street
but the west end of the block is all but bare –
Jimmy Ryan's, the Onyx, Downbeat, the Samoa,
Spotlite, The Three Deuces, The Famous Door –
all back to the dingy brownstones that stood before the War.
The only gig he can get is depping
with the Junkyard Angels at the Lone Star Café;
midway through *Close Up The Honky Tonks*
he's had enough, rips open his bag of salt peanuts
and blows them all away.

Next morning, early, two repo men with neat pony tails
sift, careful, through the ashes: "Green shoes?"
they say, perplexed. "Green shoes?"

Safeway

I like a woman who knows her way to Safeway
but who will pack me off there anyway,
a list fixed to the refrigerator door –
'wonderful lettuce', 'big dill',
'great tomatoes', 'serious bread'.
And I will tiptoe to the kitchen,
juggling misshapen bags and packages,
wallet, checked-off list and keys;
set each and everything quietly in the place
bestowed for it – as quietly as lollo rosso
wrapped in cellophane will agree to go.
But a woman who will slide her hands
across my eyes the instant I step through
the door and have me turn towards her face,
the soft grey vest across her breasts,
soft and supple sweetness of her skin.
And after we have risen from the wreck
of fallen groceries, either she or I will slide
a garlic-basted chicken from its bag, uncork
a bottle of that Merlot and take them both to bed,
sitting in the soon-to-be-sweaty whiteness
of sheets, breaking the chicken with our hands,
aware of the joy of this and each other's eyes,
the juice that runs along our fingers
and gathers in the deep spaces inside
our arms and behind our knees, waiting
to be found there later, savoured, licked away.

Seven Year Ache

"There's nothing so spiritual about being happy
but you can't miss a day of it, because it doesn't last."
Frank O'Hara: Poem ('And tomorrow morning at 8 o'clock')

for Roseanne Cash

Listening to the radio this afternoon,
thumbing through my well-worn life of Frank O'Hara,
its pink and purple annotations,
I notice *Top Hat's* on TV in time to see
Fred & Ginger shelter in that convenient bandstand
while she mimics so perfectly his routine,
and I think of the young O'Hara watching them
for the first time from those red velvet seats
at the Worcester Warner's. How he loved them!
Ginger's 'pageboy bob'; Fred's 'peach-melba voice'.
Watching them now, I hate Astaire's dinner-suited smugness,
his certainty he'll get the girl in the end.

Last night, and then again today, I'm taunted
by the bizarre easiness of dying. O'Hara at forty
knocked over by a straying jeep on the beach;
his mother, frail from hospital and drying out,
tumbling yellow roses into his grave. Such waste!
Each day we die not from love but lack of it;
the pull of your hand away from mine, the turn
of your face aside, lives lived not in hope but regret.
Whatever flowers are thrown on that fresh-turned earth
will carry with them, bright and unremarkable,
the stench of what was missed.

Valentine

Is this the way it will be?

We scrunch up against winter glass
watching for a break in the cloud
a breath of sun

This fall of water   This stand of trees
Sweet Chetsnut   English Oak

Light
like silver chainmail across the water

On the far pond the heron
unveils grey wings for flight

Last spring we sat in pale sunshine
on an outcrop of rock
      oblivious
marooned

Nine months on
we cradle china mugs   read books   and wait

Inside you
new life turns with each swelling of the tide

Blue Settee

After reading Tess Gallagher's 'Portable Kisses'

This kiss is made of remembering,
of not quite remembering enough;
this kiss deep in her pocket,
cinema tickets and small change;
the movement of her mouth that rarely
seems to mesh with his – strangely, he likes this –
the way they use their tongues.
This kiss starts at the nape of the neck
and makes a new map of the world;
moves them from the clumsy darkness
of the hall into failing sunlight
where they practise compass movements
on the bed, their way lit by candles
and Chardonnay, his tongue crossing hers
mid-ocean as she turns beneath him
and floats free; their breath sounding
an intinerary of Irish Sea, Atlantic Ocean,
and on down the coast of Maine.
Timetables. Taxis. A blue settee,
The sweep and blur of skin.
She could tell him anything.

By The Numbers

After 'Inventory' by William Corbett
from his 'Columbus Square Journal: 1974–75'

Five letters so far today, three postcards,
including one from my pal, Al, in Mexico,
hopefully writing sestinas somewhere
south of Guadalajara; a many-times sealed
brown envelope brimming with poems
badly typed yet charged with spiritual content
and the energy of God's grace and mine
to publish should I only say the word.
One apple, two bananas, several handfuls
of mixed dried fruits; four coffees,
each one stronger than the last.
My first whisky, Talisker or Highland Park,
I save for later and the first notes
of Art Pepper's keening saxophone –
Leicester it was, I saw him, eighty-one or –two,
that false summer that flared so bright
before he died – and now I sit listening to him
play *Too Close For Comfort* and waiting for you,
your key against the lock, table already laid,
sweet potato and fennel soup simmering
on the stove, five cheeses ready on the plate,
– Vignotte, Blue Stilton, Cornish Cheddar,
a stump of somewhat sweaty Feta, Raclette –
the first raspberries of the season, bought
this morning at the market, you carried
them home and hurried out again, leaving
me the task of copying the addresses,
fifty or more, from our old address book,
into something cool and trendy and sturdy enough,
hopefully, to contain all our friends, various and sundry,
including, at the last count, seven Romanians,

two Bulgarians, several Fins, the odd German,
the young poet I intend to publish from
the Republic of Moldova, numerous Frenchmen,
that woman Geoff was forever trying to get off with,
the one from Macedonia. That done, I sit out
on the balcony catching the late evening sun –
purple geraniums brought back from the garden centre,
dahlias, lobelia, richly purple and dark-veined
petunias, white impatiens to break up the colour –
my father, were he living, would have opted
for some simple daisies, marigolds,
the climbing roses he cut and trimmed
so carefully before setting on my mother's table.
How many close relatives among these addresses?
One son, two daughters, several cousins,
much removed. All day I have been dipping
in and out of books. James Schuyler's *Diaries*,
Sapphire's *Push*, Ben Sidran's *Talking Jazz*.
A week ago we moved however many
hundredweight from shelf to floor and back again:
fourteen Jim Harrisons, ten Thom McGuane,
the complete Lawrence Cathy bought me
in that white Penguin edition, each with its
small photograph, coloured and bright;
Ray Carver and Tess Gallagher, close if not
exactly side by side; Hammett, Chandler,
Elmore Leonard, Ross Macdonald, James M. Cain.
There was a time when I would count and catalogue
everything: movies, poems, plays, girls I was in love with,
girls I fancied, girls I might might one day marry,
girls I would go out with if I could.
Notebooks that went with me from the Rex, East Finchley
to the Everyman, Hampstead, the Curzon Mayfair
to the Gate, the old Electric Cinema on Portobello
to the Academy on Oxford Street, long gone.
A proliferation of Bergman and Fellini, Hawks and Ford,

the balcony of the Gaumont – or was it the Odeon? –
in Camden Town, an education, as Frank O'Hara said,
of quite another kind. Oh, Carol where are you now
with your tight sweater and pursed lips?
Fifteen, you seemed a decade older, saw the world,
clear and dangerous, with quite another eye.
Who would have thought then we would know
as little as we know now? How many friends
are living still, how many dead? My good friend,
Tom, from whom I learned so much, not least
the power of righteous indignation; Tom,
after whom my wife and I named our son,
would be the same age as me now had he lived.
Mitchum, slow-eyed and heavy-shouldered,
with his ballet-dancer's walk, has died, I see,
at sixty-nine; James Stewart, haunted still, I wager,
by the frightened beauty behind Kim Novak's eyes,
has finally succumbed at eighty-one.
I cling with not-so-quiet desperation to the years
of those active beyond their so-called time:
Harry Gold, still blowing bass sax with his
Pieces of Eight, played his first gig in 1923;
Benny Carter, soloing elegantly in New York
at eighty-nine; the list goes on.
The other night I watched Compay Segundo,
suddenly after ninety years in Cuba,
a world recording star, playing his seven-string
guitar, his leathered-face lit up by laughter
and the hope that danced on in his eyes.
There is this to do and that to do,
a dozen tasks already set, others forming in my head;
one last espresso, Veluto Nero, as we sit here,
legs and bodies stretched out along this fond settee,
talking about today, tomorrow, all the days
that come after, infinite and uncountable.

Blue Monk

Driving through Camberwell
the rain slides down black across the windscreen
and as we pass the lights for the third time
you push a cassette into place
the click and hiss of tape and then it's him:
Rhythm-a-ning. Charlie Rouse on tenor,
Sam Jones on bass, Art Taylor at the drums.
New York City, February, 1959 ...

For all the world as if he has just walked in off the street, a gas
company official, perhaps, a removal man, something humdrum;
when he sits at the piano it is as any man, unconcerned, might sit
at a park bench, ease the weight from his feet, so palpable the relief
with which he sinks into the quilted leather of the seat, his topcoat,
which he makes no attempt to undo, straining so tight across his
back one or two stitches have already snapped.

And now a scattering of applause has started up haphazardly from
around the hall; an age, still, before he eases back his cuffs, stretches
out his hands ...

The critics at this time damn his work with faint praise, another
black jazzman touring Europe, parading the same few tricks for a
handful of gold. But tonight – Rotterdam or Oslo, where doesn't
matter, this is different. Monk is on.

Audience forgotten, that oversize foot pounds down at an awkward
angle and the crowd, holding its breath, cranes forward, eager for
the fire that flares so unexpectedly, so close to the end of this life.

Inside his overcoat, under his chequered hat, Monk is lost and doesn't
care if he's never found. Doesn't give a good Goddamn. His fingers
stab at single notes, crush chords, roll with the tide then tighten down.

His hands seek and find warm spaces lost between the keys; laughter strung out along the dark like the lights of fishermen spaced along the beach, like phosphorescence on the sea, like Whistler's *Nocturne in Blue and Gold*, like the glow of radio stations long into the night.

I carry my wine to where you sit
across the room
and we stare out across this London square
these London streets
the sounds of lives departing
arriving
and when I hear draw up outside
the cab to take me home
I wonder what if, on that precipice of kitchen,
all those years ago,
instead of rinsing those last dishes in the sink
I had taken both your hands in mine
and said I would go with you
no matter where, no matter what?

Monk gets up from the piano as casually as he sat down, troubled by the memory of a promise he once made and now can neither fully remember nor forget. In the small hotel room, with a view over the air ducts and the kitchens, where he will sleep, a bottle of brandy waits, half-drunk, beside the bed.

I can never again watch your dress
fall to the floor or rest my breast
against your breast, my mouth pressed
to yours to stop it with a kiss.

C minor, F 7th, B flat –
nothing can be bluer than this.